BLUE PLANET

by Moira Butterfield • Illustrated by Jonathan Woodward

To Ian, Jack, and Gus, always ~ M.B.

For Mali and Samson, my two creative, nature-loving cubs.
May your world always be full of wonder ~ J.W.

360 DEGREES, an imprint of Tiger Tales
5 River Road, Suite 128, Wilton, CT 06897
First published in the United States 2018
Text by Moira Butterfield
Illustrations by Jonathan Woodward
Text and illustrations copyright © 2018 Little Tiger Press Ltd.
ISBN-13: 978-1-944530-96-9
ISBN-10: 1-944530-96-7
Printed in China
LT/1800/0096/0720
All rights reserved
10 9 8 7 6 5 4 3 2
For more insight and activities, visit us at www.tigertalesbooks.com

Contents

Our Blue Planet

If you are ever lucky enough to travel into space, be sure to take a look back at Earth. You will see a mostly-blue planet, hanging in the sky like a shiny marble.

Water gives our planet life.

Blue Jewel

The oceans stretch around Earth beneath the clouds. There are rivers and lakes, too. Rivers find a path between the hills to flow down into the ocean.

Floating World

Many people live on the waters of the world in specially built homes.

About 71% of Earth is covered in water.

Most of the water is salty.
The rest is fresh water or ice.

Deep Down

Underwater creatures, from giant squid to small snails, live in our huge, deep oceans. Some live so far down that they never see the sunlight.

Cloudy Sky

Even the sky is full of water, which gathers in rain clouds. Without clouds, we would not have fresh water to drink.

All Life

Water helps plants to grow and animals to survive.

Rain, Rain, Around Again

We need rain to keep our seas, rivers, and lakes filled with sparkling water. Did you know that rainwater goes around in a big circle? This is called the water cycle.

1 There is water all around you, floating in the air. It's called water vapor. You can see clouds of water vapor above a steaming kettle.

2 The sun warms the water in the seas, rivers, and lakes of the world. It makes water vapor rise up into the air.

3 The vapor rises up and up, and it gradually gets cooler. Then it begins to turn into tiny droplets.

4 The droplets bump together and join up in the sky. They get bigger and bigger and begin to form clouds.

5 The water droplets get so big and heavy that they fall as rain, back into the seas, rivers, and lakes of the world.

6 We're back where we started! That's because rain goes around and around—up into the air and back down—forever! It's the reason our planet is such a beautiful blue.

See the Seas

The world has five oceans that flow around the planet.

Arctic Ocean

North America

Europe

Asia

Atlantic Ocean

Africa

South America

Pacific Ocean

Indian Ocean

Oceania

Southern Ocean

Antarctica

Pacific Ocean

The Pacific Ocean is the largest ocean. It is bigger than all the world's land put together. Its waters are warm.

bottlenose dolphin

butterfly fish

giant clam

giant octopus

Atlantic Ocean

sea lion

sperm whale

cod

green sea turtle

The Atlantic Ocean is named after an Ancient Greek god named Atlas, who held up the sky on his giant shoulders. Its waters are cool.

Indian Ocean

The Indian Ocean has warm waters and many islands, big and small.

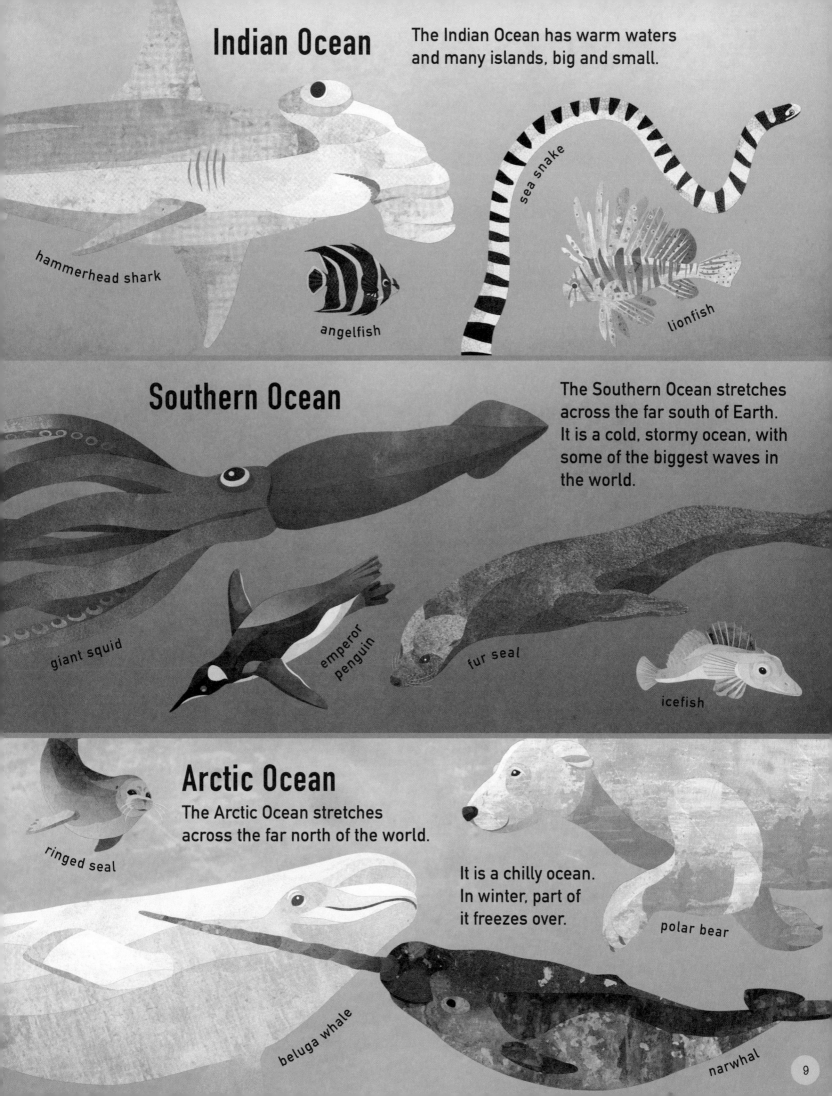

hammerhead shark

angelfish

sea snake

lionfish

Southern Ocean

The Southern Ocean stretches across the far south of Earth. It is a cold, stormy ocean, with some of the biggest waves in the world.

giant squid

emperor penguin

fur seal

icefish

Arctic Ocean

The Arctic Ocean stretches across the far north of the world.

ringed seal

It is a chilly ocean. In winter, part of it freezes over.

polar bear

beluga whale

narwhal

Tiny Big Enormous

All kinds of creatures, big and small,
make their home in the beautiful
blue oceans.

ocean sunfish

Ocean Sunfish

These bizarre-looking creatures grow
to be almost 11 feet (3.3 m)—that's
longer than an adult's surfboard.

Whale sharks
are the biggest
fish in the ocean.

Whale Shark

Whale sharks can grow to be 30 feet (9 m) long! That's
the length of three cars lined up, one in front of the other.

Leatherback Turtle

These turtles are named for their soft, leathery shells. The biggest leatherback turtles are 6.5 feet (2 m) long. That's about the size of a moped.

leatherback turtle

Pygmy Seahorse

The smallest seahorse is the pygmy seahorse. It is about the size of a grown-up's thumbnail.

0.7 inch (2 cm)

Blue Whale

These mighty whales are the largest animals that have ever lived on Earth. The biggest ones grow up to 108 feet (33 m)—that's longer than two long-distances buses parked one in front of the other.

blue whale

Great white sharks can grow to be as big as a large passenger van.

great white shark

Great White Shark

The great white shark is a fearsome ocean giant that would eat you! It can grow to a whopping 23 feet (7 m).

whale shark

My Blue Neighborhood

If you dove down beneath the blue sea, you would find a lot of different watery neighborhoods where creatures live.

Rocky Seabed

lobster

moray eel

octopus

Moray eels are the biggest eels in the world. They can grow as long as 8 feet (2.5 m).

Even the largest octopus, at 30 feet (9 m) long, can squeeze through a hole as tiny as a nickel!

Muddy Seabed

These creatures munch up pieces of food that fall down to the seabed.

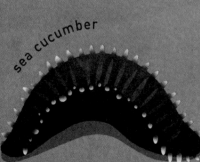

sea cucumber

There are more than 1,000 kinds of sea cucumber, of all different colors and shapes.

crab

plaice

Plaice are good at hiding in the sand.

Coral Reef

Corals are tiny sea creatures with a hard outer skeleton.

sea anemone

parrotfish

coral

clownfish

Clownfish like to live among sea anemones. They nibble the algae that grows on the reef.

butterfly fish

Deep Sea

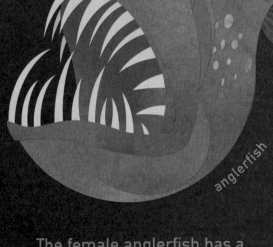

Some deep-sea fish have lights on their bodies to attract smaller fish. The little ones get eaten if they swim too close!

hatchetfish

Viperfish have scary-looking fangs to catch prey. Luckily, the viperfish is only 12 inches (30 cm) long.

anglerfish

viperfish

The female anglerfish has a light on the end of a stalk, like a fishing rod.

In and Out

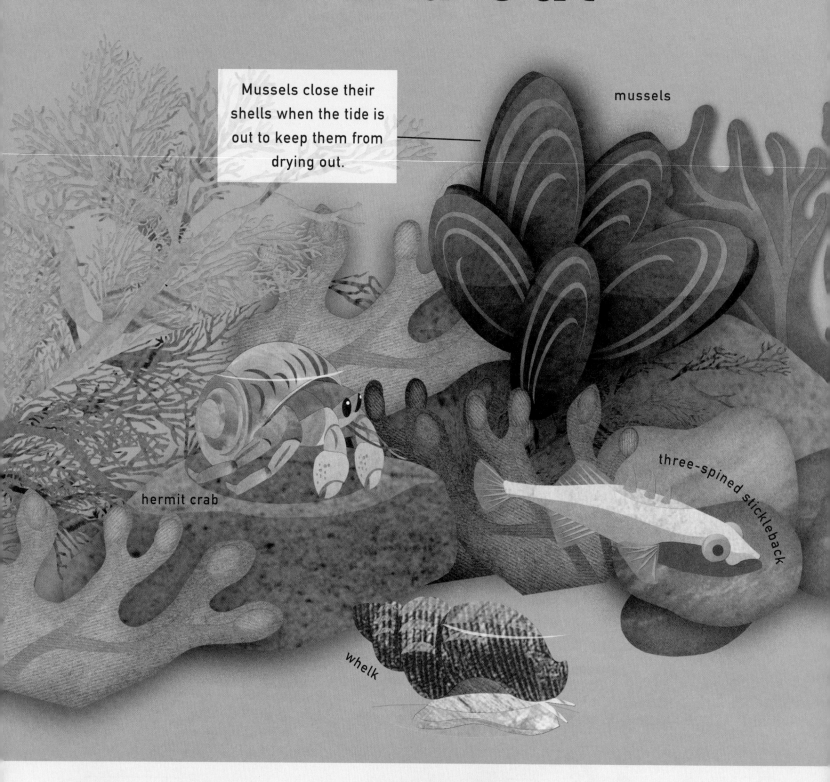

Mussels close their shells when the tide is out to keep them from drying out.

mussels

hermit crab

three-spined stickleback

whelk

Hide!

The crab must hide itself from hungry birds who would like to grab it.

It finds a safe hiding place under some seaweed in the rock pool.

The ocean has tides, which means it washes in across the shore and then washes out again, twice a day. Sea animals that live near the shore must take shelter in rock pools when the tide goes out.

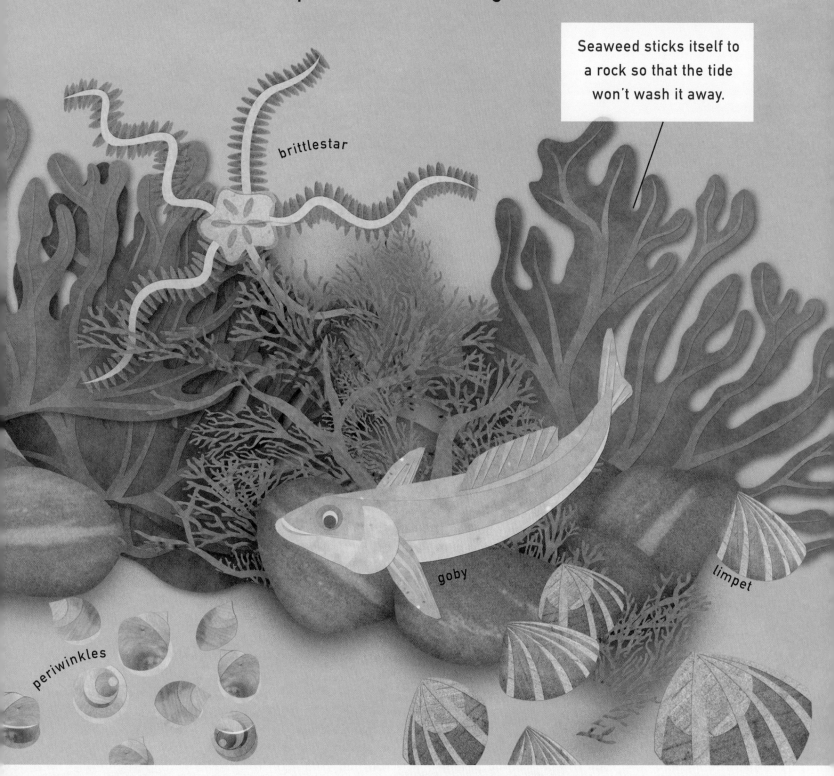

Seaweed sticks itself to a rock so that the tide won't wash it away.

brittlestar

goby

limpet

periwinkles

Finding a Home

The little hermit crab finds a shell to live inside.

When it grows, it has to leave its home to find a bigger shell.

Setting Sail

Imagine a life on the ocean waves, throwing out your fishing nets, steering your giant ocean liner, or racing in your yacht as fast as the wind will carry you. Which boat would you choose to sail on the deep, blue sea today?

Cruise Ship

A cruise ship is like a floating hotel, with all the things the passengers need for a good vacation.

Racing Yacht

The crew must be quick to change the sails to catch the wind during a race.

Fishing Trawler

Once the fish is caught, it is stored in a refrigerator inside the ship.

Speedboat

The record for the fastest speedboat ride is more than 310 miles per hour (499 kph).

Container Ship

The biggest container ships stretch to longer than four football fields and carry 20,000 containers, each the size of a big truck.

M S W

Containers carry all kinds of cargo from around the world, from toys to food to cars.

Sailing Ship

Ships like this were once used to explore the world and discover new lands.

Catamaran

Catamarans can go fast, so they are great for racing. Their top speed is more than 50 miles per hour (80 kph). A catamaran has two hulls, side by side. The crew sits in a cabin between the hulls.

The first person to sail around the world nonstop and single-handedly was Robin Knox-Johnston in 1969.

Rescue Boat

Bright colors make sure this speedy boat can be seen. The rescue crew is trained to help anyone in trouble.

RNLI

Flying Swimming Hopping

All across our planet there are rivers—tumbling and turning, splashing and flowing to the deep, blue sea. Here are some of the creatures that you would see in most rivers of the world.

Frogs Big and Small

The biggest frog in the world is the goliath frog from West Africa. It can grow bigger than a soccer ball.

Smallest Swimmer

The smallest freshwater fish in the world is called a paedocypris. It lives in the swamps of Borneo, and it's about the size of a grown-up's pinky fingernail!

Most fish hatch from eggs that are laid underwater. The fish babies are called "fry."

Big Fish

The largest freshwater fish in the world is the beluga sturgeon, found in Russia. The biggest ever found was 24 feet (7.2 m) long—about the size of a small motorboat.

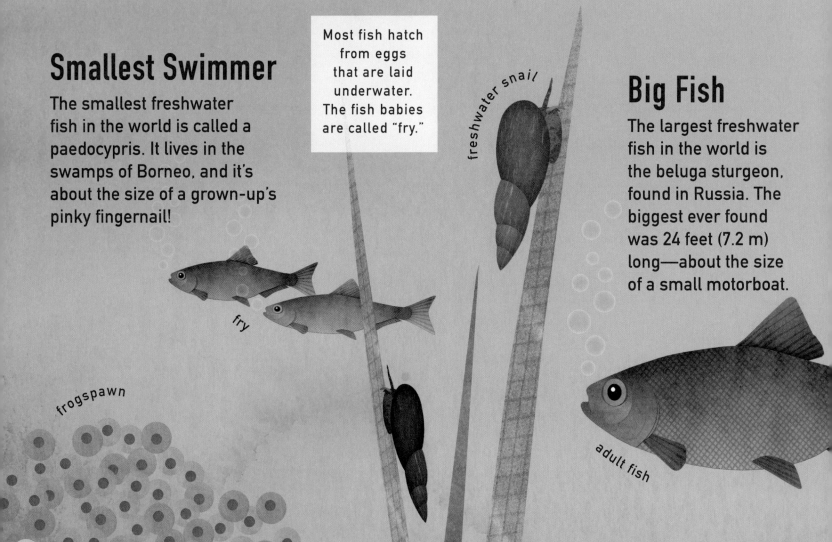

dragonfly

Dragonflies are expert fliers and can hover in midair.

Ducking for Dinner

Freshwater ducks eat animals and plants that they find underwater.

otter

duck

Otter Digger

Otters dig out hidden tunnels and safe places to sleep in the riverbank. They hunt for fish and are expert swimmers with warm, waterproof coats.

Follow the River

A mountain river changes as it travels from the place where it begins to the point where it reaches the ocean.

1 High up on a mountain, snow is melting and flowing down the mountainside. The river is born.

2 At first, the river is a little stream. Its water is fresh and cold.

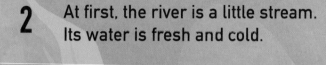

3 The river runs down the hill, tumbling over rocks.

4 The river runs, faster and faster, until it tumbles over steep rocks to create a waterfall.

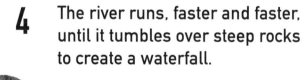

5 Down, down the river goes, growing bigger all the time.

6 It winds this way and that, gently slowing down.

7 At last, it reaches the salty ocean.

There are thousands of rivers flowing across the world, from mountains and springs to the sea.

Who Hides in the Mighty Rivers?

The world's biggest rivers twist and turn across entire countries and have many hundreds of different animals living in their depths.

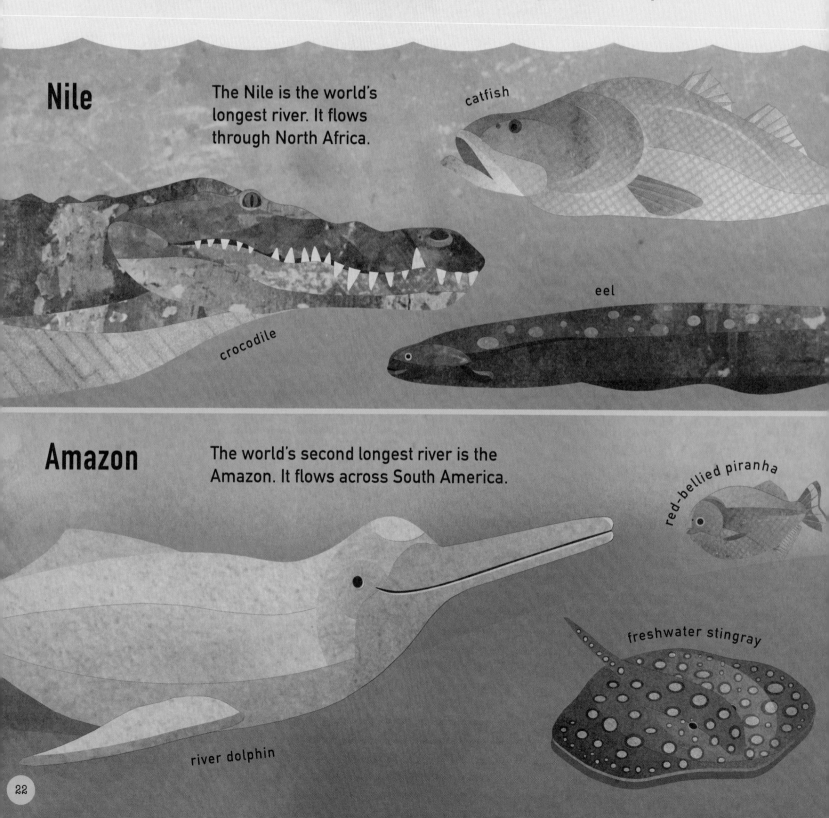

Nile

The Nile is the world's longest river. It flows through North Africa.

catfish

crocodile

eel

Amazon

The world's second longest river is the Amazon. It flows across South America.

red-bellied piranha

freshwater stingray

river dolphin

Egypt

AMAZON

China

MISSISSIPPI

NILE

South America

YANGTZE

United States

Yangtze

The world's third longest river is the Yangtze, which flows through China.

copper fish

Chinese alligator

giant salamander

walleye

Mississippi

The world's fourth largest river is the Mississippi, which flows across North America.

snapping turtle

beaver

Lands of Lakes

There are many lakes all over the world—and none of them looks the same. Some lakes started as melting ice thousands of years ago, some are fed by rivers, and some are man-made.

Lake Ontario, between Canada and the US

Some lakes are deep and wide, like seas. They even have waves like an ocean.

Visit beautiful Lake **Ontario**

SERPENTINE BOATING LAKE

LONDON, UK.

POST OFFICE LONDON

5th Jan

Some lakes are so small you could row a boat around them.

Loch Ness, Scotland

SCOTTISH • HIGHLANDS

Some lakes are the deepest, darkest blue, like ink spilled from a pot.

GREETINGS FROM SUNNY **Loch Ness**

Lake Tekapo,
New Zealand

Some lakes are
bright blue, like
the sky when the
sun shines.

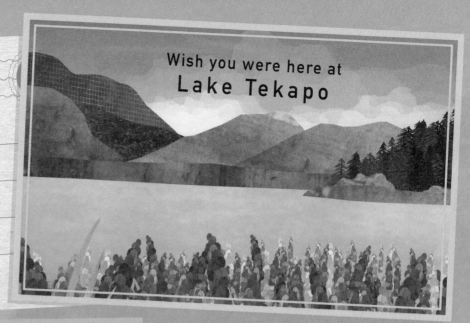

Wish you were here at
Lake Tekapo

Jasna Lake

EUROPE SLOVENIA

5th
Jan

Some lakes
are hidden away,
high on mountains.

Cheow Lan Lake,
Thailand

Some lakes are
hidden in hot,
steamy, monsoon
rain forests.

ASIA SOUTHEAST

JUNGLE LAKE

Amphibious planes can land on water and
are perfect for reaching remote areas.

Have You Ever Seen . . . ?

Some of the most bizarre-looking creatures on Earth are lake animals.

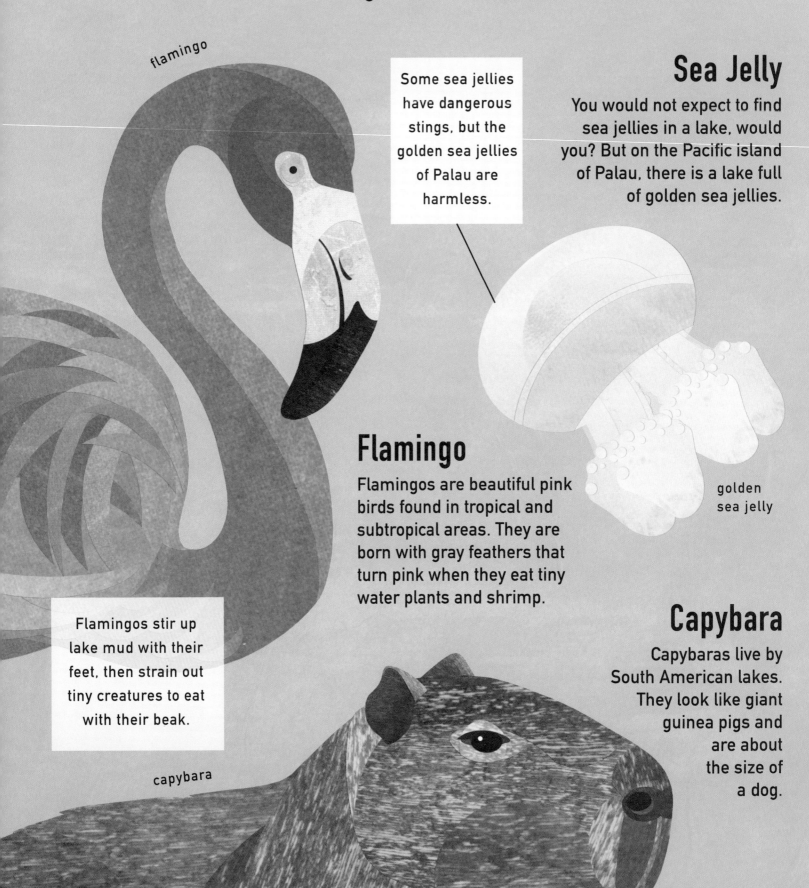

flamingo

Sea Jelly

You would not expect to find sea jellies in a lake, would you? But on the Pacific island of Palau, there is a lake full of golden sea jellies.

Some sea jellies have dangerous stings, but the golden sea jellies of Palau are harmless.

Flamingo

Flamingos are beautiful pink birds found in tropical and subtropical areas. They are born with gray feathers that turn pink when they eat tiny water plants and shrimp.

golden sea jelly

Flamingos stir up lake mud with their feet, then strain out tiny creatures to eat with their beak.

Capybara

Capybaras live by South American lakes. They look like giant guinea pigs and are about the size of a dog.

capybara

axolotl

Axolotl

The axolotl is a frog-like animal that lives in Mexican lakes. It can use its tiny limbs to walk underwater and can grow up to 12 inches (30 cm) long.

Male platypuses are venomous. They have sharp stingers on the heels of their back feet.

Platypus

The Australian platypus has a beak and feet like a duck, a body like an otter, and a tail like a beaver.

platypus

Baikal seal

Baikal seal

Roly-poly Baikal seals live around Baikal Lake in Russia. They are the only freshwater seals in the world.

At Home on the Water

Some people live on lakes and seas, where there is plenty of fish and water on their doorstep.

Floating Homes

The Uros people live on Lake Titicaca in South America. They weave floating islands from the lake reeds.

Above the Waves

The Bajau people live in wooden houses on stilts, in the sea off the coast of Malaysia. They travel around from village to village by boat.

Schools on Stilts

The lake of Tonlé Sap is in Cambodia. The buildings there are all on stilts, and the children go to school by boat. The water of the lake rises 39 feet (12 m) during the rainy season.

Beautiful Barges

Kerala in India is famous for its houseboats. These are barges that have been turned into homes and are moored on the riverbanks.

29

Wonderful Water

What would you do without water? How would you keep clean or make a drink? Luckily, in many parts of the world, water is ready to flow into your home whenever you need it. Here's how:

1 Rainwater is collected in artificial lakes called reservoirs.

2 It travels by pipes to treatment plants, where it is carefully cleaned to make it ready to drink.

3 Then it travels through pipes again, big and small, all the way to our taps.

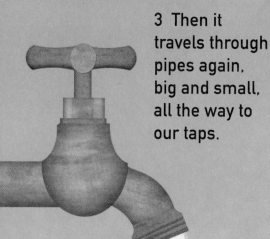

In some parts of the world, people do not have taps in their homes. They have to walk to a well—sometimes far away—to collect buckets of water.

Water is not only great for animals. People love to spend time on water, in it, and near it!

Water brings life to the world. Don't waste it. Don't spoil it. It's a sparkling treasure!

31

Index